ABOUT THE AUTH

David Mason has worked as an imr

sales training manager and has owned a restaurant. He

began writing in 1993; his first book was produced in

1996. He works in schools teaching children how to be

terribly dramatic and write stories and poems. He has

six wonderful children and a lovely wife. They live in

Norfolk in a happy, noisy house.

"Two into One" © David J. Mason 2006, Reprinted 2008
Publishing address: North Street Publishing
1 Millfield Road, North Walsham, Norfolk NR28 0EB
Telephone: 01692 406877   www.InspireToWrite.co.uk
Email: DavidMasonPoet@AOL.com

By the same author:

"Inside Out"	Poetry 1996
"Speaking Out"	Audio collection 1997
"Get a Life"	Poetry 1997; illustrations by Nick Walmsley
"Seven Summers"	Poetry 1998
"Leo's Magic Shoes"	Children's novel 1999; illustrations by Kirsty Munro. Reprinted in 2000 as "Pedro's Magic Shoes" with illustrations by Nick Walmsley
"The Great Sweetshop Robbery"	Children's poetry 2001
"Handy Andy has the Candy"	Children's poetry 2001
"Go Teddy Go"	Children's CD poetry-songs 2002
"The Elf who sang the King to sleep"	Children's fables and fairy tales 2002
"Living in another world"	Children's poetry 2003
"Teacher's Cauldron"	Children's poetry 2004
"When…"	Children's poetry 2005
"Two into one"	Children's poetry 2006 Reprinted 2008
"The White Book"	Children's poetry 2006
"Learning to Fly"	Children's novel 2007

Printed by JEM Digital Print Services Ltd
Staplehurst Road, Sittingbourne, Kent ME10 2NH
www.jem.co.uk

Poetry and Song

Mr. Mason's books

Mr. Mason's books are biologically
Sound one hundred percent bio
Degradable and natural.
Mr. Mason's pages
Are rice paper
Chocolate flavoured
Glued in Golden Syrup
Before careful binding.
When you have finished reading
You might try sharing
One of his edible books
With a close friend.
You can either read it
Or eat it together
Whatever,
Do digest the words.

Being a poet

Creativity
It's not that easy
Every bit of me heart
It takes to get arty.
The passion
It splits me brain
Gettin' dizzy
No, it's not that easy.
I feel faintly
Collapse maybe
Blood pumpin'
Wires jumpin'
Arteries thumpin'
Leaving nothin'.
No it's not easy
Creativity
Music, poetry
Thinkin' freely
Yes, it's pricey
It'll cost you dearly
Creativity
It's not that easy.

Long live the chocolate biscuit

I held a chocolate biscuit
In the palm of my right hand
Just imagine my surprise
When I heard him make a sound.
"You'll not eat me
Today," he said,
"You swallow me
And I'll be dead.
I want to be alive and free
I'm on the run, just wait and see."
So biscuit leapt onto the floor
But couldn't run through shut tight door.
"I have you biscuit now," I say.
"There is nowhere to run away"
But biscuit he will not be beaten
And says that he never will be eaten.
"No," he said, "I'll dodge and weave
You'll never catch me, wait and see,
Wait and see, you won't catch me."
He hides between the fridge and cooker.
I wait, he thinks that I'm not looking,
Out pokes his little chocolate head
Grab his body, "There!" I said.
"I have you now, I'll not let go.
I'm ready now to swallow you whole."
Biscuit he is screaming and kicking
I am hungry my lips a-licking.
"Oh have mercy, let me go!"
"No chocolate biscuit, no, no, no!"
He is shouting, "Let me out!"
Echoing within my mouth.
I swallow and I hear the sound
From deep within the sound profound.
Loud then softer, softer still,
"I don't, I don't feel so well."

Chocolate biscuit had breathed his last
His chocolate life had surely passed.
But his sweet sad voice had touched my soul
I could never again eat a biscuit, no!
And my advice to each one of you –
Think again before you do.
Come, close the cupboard, say a prayer
For chocolate biscuits everywhere
Keep them safe away from hungry children
And adults who would like to nibble them.
Don't take the biscuit, leave him be
Safely in his wrapper see!
Join the struggle, donations give
And let the chocolate biscuit live!

Snow, snow, snow, snow (for Rory)

Sense of snow sneaking
Softly, softly through winter sky
I can feel the flakes falling
All is white as I close my eyes.
There is no voice
There is no sound
But I feel the flakes
Fall to the ground
And I toss and I turn
On the fresh linen sheet
And I roll in the white
And I hide in the deep.
I snuggle for warmth
In the shell of my clothes
Curl in a ball
To fight off the cold
Of snowball whizzing
Of snowman's snow
Riding like the wind
Where the sleighmen will not go
And rolling and rolling
And rolling back home.
Leaping to the curtain
Pulling for a peak
At the blanket of white
Which snuggles the street
And the farm and the fields
And the woodlands afar
I see the flakes falling
I feel the calm.

The refugee

A stranger from another land
A refuge I can't understand.
Your open mouth
And empty words
Secrets from another world.
I fumble, I stumble
And long for my normal
You're shouting and waving
You're losing your patience.

A simple step towards me then
Help turn my world back round again.
A loving heart, a gentle hand,
Help me, slowly understand.
Talk to me of my homeland
Show me that you understand
Then my world will make more sense
I'm happy in the present tense.

"Go and see the Head"

I looked long at the sign on
The door which read
(In big bold style) "Head".
A lump in my throat
A feeling of dread
What was it that the other
Kids had said?
-You'll wish you were anywhere
Else instead
Of the room which read "Head".
I looked again anything instead
But it still said "Head", I read
Fear and dread
I'm dead
But must knock for the head
I have I've prayed.
"Come in," says the Head
And the door is pushed
And I see instead
Of a body, a head
Just a head
The head of our Head
And I wish I were
Anywhere else instead.

Before SATs

There once was a time
Called the Time before SATS
Then there was topic, English and Maths
And a large nature table
Filled with leaves, seeds
Sticklebacks, tadpoles and honey bees.
Big imaginations abounded
Stories on the radio sounded.
We were taken for walks in woods
Where we studied nothing in particular.
We pressed the leaves
Saw them fall and flutter
And felt, that light feeling of life breathing.
Before SATs all the fun in the world
Came into our classroom
And we learnt the two lessons
Childhood and freedom.
And we were never
Examined on them.

"Spider on the web"

Have you got a web site?
Said one spider to the other.
Oh no I'm not on-line yet
I'm too old to bother.
I'm not the electronic type
Don't want a mega byte.
I like to spin a yarn or two
I like old-fashioned flies
And crawling on me eight legs
Don't want a hardened disk
Or travel into cyberspace
It's just not worth the risk.
I'll not accept your email
You'll have to speak instead
BlackWidow-dot-com just won't do
Try "spider on the web".

Cheesy feet, the recipe

Socks, don't change them
Whatever you do
Feet turn rancid
In the rubber shoe
Strangle them
Don't let them breathe
Incubate, ferment-ate
Start the cheese.
Keep 'em moist
Keep 'em hot
Never remove the
Prisoner foot.
Athlete's foot
And fungus grow
A home for bugs
Between the toes.
Repeat instructions everyday
Make your cheese the natural way.
Unwrap, you find by Sunday night
The culture's done, the curd is ripe.
But take care when removing shoe
A quick exit out of the room.
Vintage cheddar, what a reek,
Gorgonzola comes next week.

Caterpillar pie

Caterpillar pie, do try!
Take a bite
Mmmm so smooth
And yet crunchy
What with the contrasting pastry
It really is so tasty.
That's the real caterpillar flavour
Something sweet, yet at the same time, bitter,
For the eater to savour.
I can, I can tell which is the head
The fleshy segments, the crackling legs.
Green juices and skin as tough as old leather
The bigger the mouthful, the better the texture.
Add herb or spice
To tease out the flavour.
(And I prefer *wild*
not *farmed* caterpillar)
My favourite? Add a little mushroom,
A clove or two of garlic -
Simmer caterpillar
Bake in a tartlet.
But do, do try,
The large caterpillar pie.
To impress the guests and dinner party,
Something different – a little chancy.
Let me introduce you too
To something bold, entirely new:
For those who prefer a lighter dish
But love that caterpillar taste.
Our very latest you simply must try
The light heavenly flutter-by butterfly pie.

The custard monster

Here comes the custard monster
Poured right into town
Most of him is yellow
Some burnt bits are brown.
The custard monster he's vanilla
He looks so smooth and sweet
Sometimes he has lumps on him
He walks with sticky feet.
See him steaming liquid hot
Or solid custard cold
He's not scared of anyone
This custard monster's bold.
He's rolling down the mountains
In a pool outside our door
He's only custard bubbles
You won't hear custard roar.
Here comes the custard monster
Creeping into town
You'll always see him smiling
You'll never see him frown.
His face so yellow and happy
The pleasant custard grin
Just leave him all your apple pies
And watch him fill them in.

Menu

Salt and vinegar (on chips)

Chips and beefburger

Burger with relish – and chips

A McWoppa, sauce – and chips

A Big One in a Big Bun – and chips

The Most Massive One with double cheese and bacon and chips

Fillet o' fish and tartare sauce with chips and sorry side salad

Chips mixed with pasta sloppy in a Bolognese sauce accompanied by garlic bread without garlic

Frozen reheated pizza with delicious cheese and tomato and mouth-watering chips

The fattest mixed grill ever bacon tomatoes sausage egg fried bread kidneys and liver – accompanied by our home-fried chips

The Steak Slab – ten pounds of prime cow cooked at your table and gently laid to rest upon a bed of chips

Hog roast – can you eat it? A whole pig with an extra large portion of chips (serves two)

Vegetarian – Chips and chips served on a bed of chips with an optional side order of French fries.

Ice-cream

Offer me olives
Beg me to eat bread.
Special spaghetti
Meat without the fat.
Salivate on salmon
Chewing on ciabatta.
Tantalize me with tomato
And cheesy roast potato.
Fingers on the fish and chips
Tomato sauce that sticks to lips.
And pick and choose the little bits
Smear the rest across the bib.
I'm not impressed with what's on offer -
There must be sweet you have to proffer.
No cake, no chocolate no other dream,
All I want is my ice-cream.
Ice-cream, ice-cream, ice-cream,
White or brown or green
But please, ice-cream
Or I'll scream
Again and again
And again.

Bathtime rules

Before bed
Comes bathtime, a good time:
Baths are not for bathing
But for swimming in.
Bubbles simply must abound,
Soap moustaches and beards
Shall be worn.
Water must be hand warm
And hair washing
Must not be done
Under any circumstances.
Half the water in the bath
Shall be splashed
On to the surrounding floor
And adults placed
In a room next door.
Not less than two
To take to the tub
And pulling the plug
Must be done
At intervals
Before end of bath
And beginning of bedtime -
A bad time!

Biscuit barrel

Who's been at the biscuits?
It was not I
Who picked out all the chocolate ones
And left the rest to die.
Who's been at the biscuits?
There's only plain ones left.
Who's nibbled all the nice bits?
Who's the icing thief?
Who's been in the biscuits?
Let me see your mitts
I don't know how it got there
But the chocolate lay in bits
Upon the palm of my hand
So she knew I was the one
Who'd been at the biscuits
'Cos biscuit-eating's fun.

Two Penguin biscuits

Two Penguin biscuits
Each has a wrapper
One gold, one green
Colour shouldn't matter.
Two Penguin biscuits
With gold or green wrapper
But the choice that you make
Does seem to matter.
Two Penguin biscuits
What's wrong with the wrapper?
It's not gold it's green
And to my mind it matters.
Two Penguin biscuits
It doesn't matter
There's chocolate hiding
Beneath the wrapper.
Two Penguins biscuits
I want the gold wrapper
It's the colour that counts
Not the chocolate that matters.
Two Penguin biscuits
I won't have the green
I don't care for the chocolate
That's sandwiched between.
One Penguin biscuit
It doesn't matter
But I'll eat the biscuit
You chew the wrapper.

How to handle a bad dream

Rule No.1
When having a bad dream
It's important to remember
The shadows you made up inside your head
Aren't real, like pictures on paper.

Rule No.2
But if you can't remember
And the shadows are real like witches
Then perhaps you would like to consider
One of the following switches.

Rule No.3
Switch to self control
And the baddies stop the chase.
You are rescued by lots of good goodies
With kind smiles and friendly face.

Rule No.4
If switch to self control won't work
Then press on the auto alarm.
Wake up and cuddle your pillow
Breathe deeply until you are calm.

Rule No.5
If the auto alarm won't function
Shout as loud as you can in your dream
And hope that your parents come running
At the terrible sound of your scream.

Rule No.6
If shouting turns to silence
Try to sleepwalk your way out of trouble
And find someone else to sleep next to
And give them a lovely warm cuddle.

Like me the way I am

You were nasty,
Pinched me hard,
Wouldn't let me join in
Your games in the playground.
Told lies about me,
Ganged up on me,
Made me lonely,
Laughed at me
So that I never want to see you
Or ever go to school again.
You turned the world against me
And I did nothing wrong
Except for being myself.
You didn't like that
And everyone else who
Doesn't like me
The way I am
Has the same problem -
And it's yours.

The handhold

I caught sight of an old man
In a souped-up invalid car.
Wow I'd like to have a go
In that, I thought
But then I don't want to
Be crippled and old.
I finished first in three races on Sports Day.
I'm bright and I'm young and I'm bold.
He looks sad and twisted
And full of pain.
He looks like he'd like to
Be young again.
As I worried about the state of his body
Along comes a girl about my age and slowly
She squeezes both his hands, gently does it
And all the age and pain rush out from him.
There is electricity in the air,
Hope has beaten off despair.
I expect to see a young prince
Arise from his invalid car
And show us what he's really like:
Young and able, handsome and smart.
Nothing happens, he sits quite still
But a smile swims across his face –
His granddaughter, her handhold, time and space.

Sprouts

I'll tell you what's the problem
With the humble brussel sprout
As soon as you have swallowed him
He's desperate to get out.
He finds his way to secret places
He hides within my gut
And then he starts his fermentation
That ends with fut-fut-fut!
What's that smell?
Who on earth was that?
Was it Mum or brother, sister,
Dad or dog upon his mat?
My face is crimson red
They know who's done the deed
But it wasn't due to indigestion
Brought on by sweetie greed.
No, it was the evil one
With darkest leaves of green
And a sour heart of sadness
With dark fibre in between.
They overcook him in the pan
And turn him into slush
He slithers up and down my throat
A monstrous mash of mush.
Everybody I know hates him
Old Greeny has no friends
Except for healthy Mums and Dads
Who say our life depends
On doing just as we are told
And playing our sprouty part
But we all know what the truth is
That sprouts they make you ill.

Snail and slug salad

You will need
A soft fresh green lettuce
Soaked in dawn dew
The half chewed variety
With holes in will do.
The best leaves are those
Which are crawling with life
Don't wash out the flavour
Don't scrape with a knife.
Now place in the mouth
Sauce of silvery trail
Left by our slug
And his good friend the snail.
The stuff it is slimy
And sticky to swallow
But then comes the tough bit
The chewing to follow
But the snail's shell is tough
And I prefer to suck it
And after the slug skin
You will need a bucket.

A poem about wrestling

Haven't you got anything about wrestling?
Was the next question
I have poems on football
-Ner!
A boy exploding because he ate too
Much chocolate?
-Ner!
A nasty, very nasty pet rat
(Well he considered that)
-Ner!
Tortuous tales of bad dreams, nightmares
He stares and stares
-Ner!
I'm running low, what else containeth
The poet's portfolio?
I should say, "I'm a successful poet you know,"
And leave it at that
But the lad – he looks dead set on
What he wants.
The poet tries again.
I've got a good lads one – a teacher with a gun!
Sounds like it could be fun
But
-Ner!
That's it, I'll close the whole
Session with a joke.
"I dunno I've written hundreds of poems
On every subject known to childkind.
Still no poem on wrestling
"I guess I must have failed the test eh?"
-Yer!

Heap big tree

Heap
Big tree
With
Heap
Big knees.
Hear the
Cheep cheep cheep
Of
Little birdies
Hiding in
A
Thousand leaves.
Please please
Save our trees
And his knees
And the birdies
And the leaves
And not forgetting
The honey bees.
If you like all of these
Don't chop them down - go plant a tree!

Mrs. Bottomley

Class, your new teacher, Mrs. Bottomley.
Strange sort of name, I'm sure you'll agree
And me I sniggered quite naturally.
"Please do tell us what you find so funny"
But I didn't couldn't wouldn't dare
Face Mrs. Bottomley, it wasn't fair
To have her call herself such a name -
Not me but her bottom that was to blame.

Things that go bump

Things that go
Bump in the night.
Ghosts and robbers
They give me a fright.
A squeaky floor
A creaking door
The heavy breathing
And someone screaming.
I can't see
In the scary black.
My heart in my mouth
I can't put it back.
Then all of a sudden
A terrible bump
And my brother has fallen
Out of the top bunk.

Muffin

Hey Muffin
You're nothing
But blueberry stuffin.
Muffin was huffin
And Muffin was puffin
Muffin was ready for a fisty cuffin
A little bit of muffin-duffin
I'm sorry Muffin
About the stuffin
It's nothing, said Muffin
Only bluffin.

The sun and the moon

When the sun drops below the horizon
And he tries to get some sleep
Imagine his irritability
With that metabolic heat.
I think of his relief
When he climbs back in the sky
And cools himself in the passing breeze
Whilst burning you and I.
I wouldn't like to be the sun
I'd rather be the moon
Smiling there in the clear cool heavens
Or wrapped in a cloudy cocoon.

Creation

On the first day God made kids.
On the second day God made furry bunnies,
cuddly cats and fluffy dogs
For the children to play with.
On the third day He made chips
And on the fourth vanilla and later chocolate ice-
cream.
God saw all this was good
And He wanted the kids to have more fun and
So invented swings and slides on the fifth day.
On the sixth day He made bunk beds and
comfortable duvets
So that the kids could rest with Him on the
seventh day.
On that day He was resting but set His alarm
clock incorrectly.
On waking God became restless -
It was then He made His first and only mistake,
Teachers and parents.

Cockroach

Cockroach in your knickers
It's not an idle threat.
I wait with the cockroach in my hand
You stand with bated breath.
I feel his feelers feeling
I see his cockroach grin
I imagine what he'll feel like
Crawling o'er your skin.
You scream at me
You wouldn't do
And I reply I would.
You couldn't do you challenge me
And I reply I could.
Do it then, you call my bluff
And I am moving in.
You realise that I'm not kidding
And turn and start to run.
I am chasing, you will lose
I know I am the faster
And now I have you in my grasp
I take the cockroach down your pants
Er - now I've dropped a clanger,
Of the cockroach there's no sign,
Now I know he's not in yours
As I feel him crawl through mine.

Autumn

Chilly Autumn calls on spider's spun door
Wet webs, crystal tears sparkling
Pulls gossamer threads to the floor.
Slyly spider sits it out – till morning sun
Liquid gold melts, pours so sleeping
Flies are enmeshed – and spider has won.
Spider idly feeds on Autumn's fare
Sticky feet tread silky maze
Deep breath drink down October's air.

Spider scuttles, hedgehog snuffles amongst deep mould
Crunch and creak, crackle
Leaves missing, branches twisting, fingers cold.
Dropped dark brown fuels on carpet floor
Spiky-cased conkers shiny
Blood red river fermenting fruit fall.
Apples are to cider, blackberries cooked to pie
Peck and pick the bounty
Sloes are to gin, grape into wine.

Ghostly blanket of morning mist wraps
Below dew glistens in watery yellow
Crystals or diamonds, leaden sky traps
Short days, sadness, slide towards winter
Dampens our fading spirits
Homeward to fire and flaming red clinker.
Armies of sentry soldier birds migration begun
Rigid, still as statues
The last of summer's song is sung.

What I want

I'm the child whose eyes
Beg for the clasp of your arms
For your crushing strength
Making warm my bones.
The nest you make
Tells me that you
And you alone
Will keep me from all harm,
Will tell me I am
Such a special
Cozy cared for individual.
But beware your strength
You might break me
Leave me lonely
Lost and lacking
If you and your love
Send me packing.
No idea of the power you hold
Tell me each new day
You love me
Don't tell me I've been told.

'Bout an alien

Wrote this story 'bout an alien
He had eight long arms
And his arms they were flailin'
Eyes on long stalks – typical Martian.
Well alien gets out his zapper gun
Me, I'm no chicken, but I start to run
Until I remembered I had one,
A laser-powered zapper gun.
Here you Martian try this for fun
And I set my laser to Martian-stun
But Martian laughs cos' he knows who's won
You can't touch an alien with a laser gun.
I had no choice, I had to run
From an alien and his zapper gun
And I don't know if you've been chased by one
But an angry alien - well it's not fun
And the bullets they fly from his zapper gun
Is my little life over and done?
Then the worse thing happens – there's two, not one
And its double trouble with alien gun.
They're chasing me everywhere under the sun
All I can do is run and run
And this story is rambling on and on
And my story has nowhere left to run
And me and my story we're done.
And that's the end or so it would seem
And then I woke up, it was all a dream...
...Says teacher – Thanks a lot for the fun
'Bout the alien and his zapper gun.
But please don't write another one.
No, please don't write another one.

Good morning everybody

Good morning everybody
Good morning Mr. Poet
I've written a poem everybody
Good for you Mr. Poet
It's a new one everybody
Well let's hear it Mr. Poet
Are you ready everybody?
We're ready Mr. Poet.
Monday morning I came to school
And said "Good morning everybody" as usual.
The end of Monday came very soon
And I said to everybody "Good Afternoon".
But then I had to change it
I had to rearrange it
Put some meaning in it
Give some feeling to it.
Here goes -
Good morning everybody!
Afternoon everyone!
Good morning everybody!
Let's make it a lively one.
Scream it, shout it
Let-it-all-out it
Should sound exciting
Set your pulse racing!
Oh hear it again
Enthusiasm meeting
Hearts set on fire
Spiritual greeting.

The Bogey Man
(To the tune of "The Muffin Man")

I think I've seen the bogey man,
The bogey man, the bogey man,
I think I've seen the bogey man,
He lives in Ludham town.

I think I've seen the bogey man,
The bogey man, the bogey man,
I think I've seen the bogey man,
He lives inside our house.

I think I've seen the bogey man,
The bogey man, the bogey man,
I think I've seen the bogey man,
He sits upon our couch.

Oh guess who is the bogey man,
The bogey man, the bogey man,
Oh guess who is the bogey man,
I guess he is my dad.

He picks his nose, thinks I can't see,
Thinks I can't see, thinks I can't see,
He picks his nose, thinks I can't see
The green upon his hand.

And your Dad's are all bogey men,
They're bogey men, they're bogey men,
Yes your Dad's are all bogey men
In this grown-up bogey land!

The Terrible (Forty)-two's

In a posh restaurant last night,
My wife had to shove the main course in my
mouth – tight.
Even then I ate less than half
And threw some at the waiter – for good
measure.
I blew bubbles in my expensive wine,
Insisting on a straw and what's more
Knocked a couple of bottles over
Pushing my plate towards the waiter:
"I don't want it, I don't want it!"
I screamed and banged my fists first
And then my head on the white linen table
And deliberately embarrassed my wife as much
As I was able.
My wife explained to our two guests,
"He's tired and irritable he's not like this
All the time.
He's normally very well behaved but he didn't
sleep
This afternoon."
"Ah yes, The Terrible Forty-two's, we've all been
there."
And our guests nod their guestly heads
And smiled very nicely at me.
I wasn't looking, I was staring at the floor
At the cutlery I had deliberately dropped there.
The staff tried their best
They brought me picture books to colour
And strapped a bright balloon to the back
Of my chair.

My wife promised me,
"Pudding will soon be here, dear.
Come on, cheer up,
Let's have a smile shall we.
I wonder just what it will be.
Let's have a look, shall we?"
And my wife read out twenty-seven
Puddings very patiently
And my expression did not change
And I looked awful glum
Said I didn't like any of them – not one.
Our guests tried again.
"Come on David, you like chocolate don't you?
Lovely chocolate, yum yum on your tongue."
I shook my head and didn't look at them.
"Will you have some ice-cream then?
After five long minutes I mumble I will
And the waiter brings me the house special
Flake and sauces, hundred and thousand
The biggest and the bestest
An ice-cream to be proud of.
I don't smile, I don't want
Them to know I'm terribly happy
And take tiny little spoonfuls very quietly.
I'm finished, I'm bored,
I want to leave now and scowl,
Make them get a move on,
Give them a good dose of indigestion.
My wife smiles apologetically
Burps and pays the bill
And turns with me out the door
Says a hurried good-bye to our visitors.
She has to carry me

The short distance home
Tucks me up in bed
I sleep like the dead
Looking lovely so serene
Forty-two and she dreams
That tomorrow when I'm forty-three,
Tomorrow being my birthday,
The Terrible Forty-two's will quietly disappear
An end to the screaming, shouting, tears
A brand new beginning
A start, a better life
For forty-three year Mr. Mason
And his understanding wife.

Wonder Stuff

Sensational – it's
The new breakfast cereal
Go on, stuff it!
You can't get enough of it.
This world's tough
This world's rough
You need Stuff!
The lighter puff
Full of ruff – age.

If you've had enough
Then Stuff's the stuff
Gives you puff
To face the rough
And tough
Of today's dizzy
Busy world.
Be prepared
Don't bluff it
Just say – Stuff it!

Dennis and the donkey

Dennis impressed
In his string vest
Long grey socks
Handkerchief head
Deckchair bound
Beetroot red
Dennis comes here every year
Big chip belly, bottles of beer
Dennis in slow motion
Shimmering lump of suntan lotion.
Says Denise, "Our Dennis,
You're a proper potato.
Ger off your bottom
And put it on Pedro!"
The donkey, the latest attraction
Four strong legs
And a promise of action
Dennis depressed
In his string vest
Mutters, "I could do with a lift."
"Well get on the donkey, shift!"
Shouts Denise in desperation
To Dennis – potato, fruit of frustration.

Then...
Tangle of seaweed, foam and splash
Dennis and donkey cut quite a dash.
Hooves a-pounding his mad eyes gleaming,
Nostrils flaring, bold sun beaming
And Dennis? Surely he's dreaming
 But no, over they go!

They jumped the first windbreak
The second, third and fourth
Pedro the crazy is running his course.
He's taking on deck chairs
He comes up to the last
Over the groynes and killer wave
The pier he leaps in a flash.
Past glittering stars
Up over the moon
Re-entering Earth's
Atmosphere very soon.
And falling, falling
Back down to the sand
The people are cheering
The sound of brass band.
Oh Dennis you hero!
You have done us proud
Hear them all clapping
Just look at the crowd!
And Denise says that
Dennis is not a potato
There's no-one more braver
Than he who rode Pedro.
Pedro he neighed
Said he was impressed
With his rider, his long socks
And old string vest
Slimline Dennis still comes here each year
Salad and suchi, no chips or beer
And Dennis he is the latest attraction
Bottom on Pedro, promise of action.

Sheep

Baa-baa bright sheep
He's nobody's fool
The others looked at his coat
And began to ridicule.
Ha ha Baa-baa!
Just look at you
You've got a black coat
And that just isn't cool.
Baa-baa simply nodded
He took all the flack
I'm an individual
'Cos I'm wearing black.
You is all the white sheep
Lookin' all de same
You think you're something special
But you don't have your own brain!

Baa-baa he says
The same the
World through
You gotta think for yourself
Not what the others do.
What you is wearin'
And what you say
The music and the politics
You go your own
Way.
Don't be a baa-baa
White sheep
Do not sell your soul
And be like everybody else
Wearing the same wool.
It's better on the outside
Not running with the pack
Forget about the white ones
And get on with being black.

Into the sea

The sun is up
It's awful nice
Off to the beach
I don't think twice
I'm feeling good
It's looking fine
I want to do
This all the time

Chorus:
Into the sea
Please come with me
It's so lovely
You can be free
Into the sea
Please come with me
You can be free
- All you have to do is take my hand

I'm on the sand
Sun bathing's hot
Some like it hot
But I do not
I'd rather cool
I like a swim
The water's blue
So come on in

Chorus

We like to laugh
And splash about
We love to surf
We love to shout
We like to dive
Into the swell
We haven't drowned
We're doing well

Chorus

Then we plunge
Into the deep
And we are kick-
-Ing with our feet
Our crawling arms
They move us on
Here it comes
The ho-ri-zon

Chorus

We're on the beach
Sun bathing's good
Some like to starve
But I like food
After a swim
I'm licking lips
It's time to fill
Me up with chips

Chorus

So now we're off
We're going home
The sun is down
The swimming's done
It's time for bed
It's time for sleep
Tomorrow – where?
Back to the beach!

Chorus

Yeah to the beach
We love the beach
Ba ba ba dap bap n'do dah!
Ba ba n'bap
Bap ba dap n'do bap
With a bap bap bap bap ba
Ba fap n'bo bap
With a bap
Diddly-dee diddly-dee
Ba dap boo!

The mermaid

A mermaid in a rock pool,
I found her hiding there
Underneath a forest of straggly seaweed
Making ribbons in her hair.

The sea was miles out from shore
Left her high and dry
And as I bent a little lower
I heard the mermaid cry.

"I'm shrinking by the second
That's why I shed a tear.
If I stay here very much longer
I shall surely disappear."

"How is it I can help you?
What is it that you need?"
"I need the depths of yonder sea,
The food on which I feed."

I dipped fingers in the rock pool
And gently picked her out.
Strode on and on far out from shore
To where the waves they sing and shout.

And though the swell was high
And the water crashed on sand,
I gently let her out to sea
Just as she had planned.

Some years later I sailed
Upon that self same sea
In a mighty craft full of precious cargo
Bound for the West Indies.

But a terrible storm it blew up
And washed me from the deck
And I watched the ship sink 'fore my eyes
As I clung on to the wreck.

When I couldn't cling on much longer,
Not in that icy swell,
And the cloud of death came over me
And my body it was still

My lungs were full of water,
My heart was full of pain.
I said my last goodbyes to all,
I'll not see you again.

Then just as I was finished,
I was hoisted from the ice
And carried miles to safety
To the shores of paradise.

The mermaid she had saved me
And bore me to the isle
And set me down on the golden sand,
Left me with a smile.

She told me that for certain
One good turn deserves another
And since I'd saved her life that day,
I'd always be her brother.

A passenger steamer picked me up,
I found my way back home.
Now I always check in rock pools
For mermaids left alone.

Rock pool

Barnacles bashed out a bluesy beat
The octopuses stampin' their sticky feet
Molluscs with maracas were making their sound
Ragworms shakin' under the ground

Anemones then added to the thrills
They opened their mouths and showed their frills
Prawns played hard on the lead guitar
On the rhythm section starfish was a star

Come on down to the rock pool
The sun's hot above but the water's cool
Everyone will wear a smile to welcome you
So dive on in to the rock, rock, rockin' pool

Limpets sucked hard but stuck to the stone
A mermaid danced to the tune all alone
Fish swam in circles a beatin' their fins
The angel fish a-fluttering their angel wings

Seahorses galloping along the sand
Larvae shake a leg to the sound of the band
The snail his eyes are out on a stalk
And the crab he's a shuffling with a sideways walk

Come on down to the rock pool
The sun's hot above but the water's cool
Everyone will wear a smile to welcome you
So dive on in to the rock, rock, rockin' pool

Then the sea joins in the waves they start to roll
Till next low tide to hear the rock pool.

Come on down to the rock pool
The sun's hot above but the water's cool
Everyone will wear a smile to welcome you
So dive on in to the rock, rock, rockin' pool

Living in another world

Chorus:
Come along with me
Come along
Come this way and see
Come along
Come along with me
Come along
Come this way and see

I'm checkin' out the groove
In the playground one day
When along comes a bein'
He strange I'll say.
He got a green body and a rubbery face
He don't look like he come from this place
He interplanetary he out of space
He says he not from the human race.

Chorus

Giving me the nod he say –
You want to go?
I say yeah I
Be leavin' this school.
He says step into this shining jewel
You don't look like nobody's fool
You don't want to play by the rules
You look like you is smart and cool.

Chorus

I'm drivin' this spaceship
Look at all the dials!
Everything is space-age
It's all computerised.
We're travellin' at a million miles an hour
Weavin' and dodgin' the meteorite shower
We got the crystals, yeah we got the power
This here is brave, no place for the coward.

Chorus

We land on the planet
I meet all his friends
They're smilin' I'm shakin'
Their slimy green hands.
They say I am special you know I'm a mate
They want me to stay they think I'm so great
So I won't be goin' home at this rate
I'm thinkin' that being here is just fate.

Chorus

And now I have all my
Friends with me
They moved to this planet
We're one big family.
We're all so happy in another galaxy
Livin' with the aliens that's where we want to be
Old planet earth seemed so dull to me
If you want a future here's where you ought to be.

Chorus

You got to be ready (Zebedee's song)

Well boys and girls
Here's the lesson for you
You'd better start doin'
What you really ought to
You got to be friends in the classroom see
Respect your teacher whoever they may be
Don't get fightin' and don't you bully
Forget the others and listen to me.

Chorus:
You got to be ready
You got to be good
You got to do all the things that
You know that you should
You got to be ready
You got to be nice
'Cos God he sees everything
Yeah he got big eyes
Oh God he sees everything
He got big eyes.

Now listen to me
And copy yeah
You mustn't be greedy
And you have to be fair
The countries they have to share out the wealth
We have to think of others forget about ourselves
All start thinkin' 'bout equality –
How you doin? Forget about me!

Chorus

There's too much hate
In the world today
Some people are aggressive
And some are just afraid
It does not matter 'bout the colour of your skin
What you believe and the clothes you dress in
You must accept what the other man say
Don't you dare force him to change his way.

Chorus

Now money is the root
Of all evil they say
Chasin' after money
Well there's a price to pay
You just have enough for your basic need
Don't' you succumb to that evil greed
Keep it simple you won't want more
With a little spirit you can never be poor.

Chorus

Now let's all work
For a better place
A new kinda world
To put a smile on our face
Contentment, hope and love and peace
An end to the greed to the modern disease
Walk with nature and set yourself free
Think for yourself who you want to be.

Chorus

Zebedee

Boom boom (da ba-da ba-da ba)
Zoom zoom (chick a-boom chick a-boom)
Zebedee comes cleaning down our street
Vroom vroom, vroom, vroom
Broom broom, broom a-broom-broom-a-broom
Zebedee he is the greatest sweep!

Zebedee he's someone
That you would like to meet
He always wears a smile
When he' cleaning up our street
Some folks say he's dumb and
That he never went to school
But that's a nasty rumour
He's clever and he's cool.

Zebedee has three degrees
A PHD or two
Collecting all our rubbish
That's what he wants to do
I don't want an office
No dull desk job for me
I prefer the outdoors
And this clean philosophy.

He says:
I don't care much for money
I like this simple life
Somewhere to live, something to eat
Six kids and a wife
Blue sky above the dreadlocks
Soft earth beneath my feet
The chatter of those people
The birdsong - tweet, tweet, tweet.

I got time for dreaming
I can sing a song
You can come and play with me
You can sing along
I've written me a few books
Stories inside my head
Yeah if you want a good time
Come listen to ol' Zeb.

We say:
Zebedee you're wonderful
There's something about you
Always friendly and content
Enjoying what you do
You're an eco-warrior
You're helpin' save this world
The best example on the street
For every boy and girl.

He says:
One last verse for everyone
A special plea from me
Something that you all could do
To please ol' Zebedee
Hey don't drop you litter!
Put it in that bin
Yeah you can join ol' Zebedee
And save the world with him!

Dandelion

I want to pick a dandelion
I love to play the game
I try to breathe in deeply
And blow back out the same

I blow like a tornado
At the dandelion white
The parachutists tremble
But hang on very tight

Chorus:
Dandelion
Flying so high
Dandelion
Up in the sky

But I'm not going to give in
I'll launch them, wait and see
And the next breath they are flying
Away across the fields

They float out on the air
And fall on foreign ground
The dandelion secretive
He never makes a sound

Chorus

He throws his parachute off
And digs a little hole
And hides there for a while
Safe in his new home

The next time that you see him
His yellow flowers shine
Then the parachutes are made
As the flowers start to die

Chorus

I want to pick a dandelion
I love to play the game
I try to breathe in deeply
And blow back out the same

The dandelion – a story
To some he's just a weed
But if you take the time you'll see
He's a famous flying seed.

Chorus

CHOCOLATÉ!
(Say "Chocolatay" - Spanish for chocolate)

Any size or any shape
Chocolate made for me
And when I'm eating chocolate
I sing this song you see:

Chorus:
Chocolat-ay! chocolat-ay! chocolatay para mi,
Si, chocolat-ay, chocolat-ay, chocolatay para ,
Chocolatay para, chocolatay para mi - cha-cha-cha!

Try me with the dark
Give me the milk
Rough and ready cooking chocolate
Or Galaxy smooth silk.

Chocolate full of almonds
A nut in every bite
Give me heavy chocolate man
Or Aero chocolate light.

Chocolate with the coconut
Chocolate with the mallow
Or how about a toffee filling
You suck to death before you swallow.

I buy it from our sweet shop
I purchase it abroad
It doesn't matter where you are
For chocolate just one word:

Chorus

Chocolate in the playground
Chocolate back at home
Chocolate breakfast, lunch and dinner
And often in between.

Chocolate in good company
Chocolate on its own
Chocolate under bedclothes
Tucked up in bed alone.

Chorus

Chocolate whilst I'm living
Chocolate till I die
And afterwards in Heaven
In a chocolate laden sky.

Yes choco-late in this life
And chocolate in the next
As long as there is chocolate
You can do without the rest.

Chorus

Chocolate for the Muslims
For Christians and all
Don't bother with religion
Come share a chocolate ball.

Yes chocolate will save mankind
If there is a nuclear war
Someone somewhere in a bunker
Lives on chocolate bars.

Chorus

Poo on your shoe

When you're out on the street
Keep a watch on your feet
What you gonna do
About the - poo on
Your shoe?

When you're running down the road
Check out the brown load
What you gonna do
About the - poo on
Your shoe?

When you're keeping goal
Keep an eye on your sole
What you gonna do
About the - poo on
Your shoe?

When you're home again
Don't let the carpet stain.
Parents mad at you
Tell them it's not true,
Some dog, somewhere else
Put the poo on your shoe.

Ah-1-2, ah1-2-3-4
What you gonna do about the
Poo on your shoe?
DOO-DOO-DOO-DOO
Poo on your shoe?
DOO-DOO-DOO-DOO
Poo on your shoe?
DOO-DOO-DOO
What you gonna do about the
Poo on your shoe?
The poo, poo, poo on your shoe.
The poo, poo, poo
O-ONNNNN
YOUR SHOE-OOOOOOOOOOOOOOOOO!
Thank you and goodnight!

OH NO, MOS-QUI-TO!

Oh no, Mos-qui-to!
Buzzing round your head
You know that sound
It's the fizzy little creature
Flying all around.
Oh no, Mos-qui-to!
But when's he gonna stop
Where's he gonna land?
May be on my leg
May be on your hand.
Oh no, Mos-qui-to!
When I turn the light on
You're nowhere to be seen
May be you're imaginary
May be in a dream.
Oh no, Mos-qui-to!
Back in the dark
You're out again
I hear you flapping
About me and then
Oh no, Mos-qui-to!
I feel you crawl
On the inside of my ear.
I take aim silently
Then THWACK! You disappear.
Oh no, Mos-qui-to!
I'm too tired
To bother any more
I hope you cannot sleep
As you listen to me snore.
Oh no, oh no, oh no,

Oh no, Mosquito, Mosquito, Mosquito, Mosquito.
I wake up in the morning
Turn on all the lights
You've been all night a-partying
I'm a mass of mozzy bites.

Handy Andy

Chorus:
Handy Andy's got the candy
Handy Andy has the fries
Handy Andy has the cola
He's the all-American guy!

Andy lived at home with his mum and dad
In an old grey room in a block of flats
I've had enough of this he said one day
I'm packing my bags for the US of A!

Chorus

He sailed in a ship 'cross the big wide sea
Said my oh my would you look at me!
Who could have guessed, who would have known
Hey California I'm comin' home

Chorus

Andy lived in 'Frisco with a hippy chick
Learned how to look cool and how to act slick
How to use all that American talk
Elevator, cookie – sidewalk

Chorus

Andy thought he'd better have his mouth done
Everyone in the States has a big white one
Polish your teeth give them cheesy grin
A mouth full of metal pop some chewing gum in

Chorus

Andy got so rich, Andy got so smart
I love the USA stamped upon his heart
The President's picture hung above his bed
The dollars going round and round in his head

Chorus

But there's a few things that poor Andy forgot
Started him thinking this place ain't quite as hot
I miss neat little England and her island ways
Cute little England and the English dames

Chorus

Now Andy's safe and snug in his English home
Two lovely kids, a wife – he is never alone
There's a picture of Her Majesty above his head
And every night he takes his English dictionary to bed

Handy Andy's got the candy
Handy Andy has the fries
Handy Andy has the cola
He's the all-American,
All-American
All-American guy!

Go Teddy!

Says Teddy to me - you know my life it's not right
I'm sleeping all the day and I'm sleeping all the night
I've got to move out to where the future's bright
Under the glare of the disco light.

Chorus:
I said go!
Go Teddy go go go!
Yo Teddy yo yo yo!
Go Teddy go go go!
Yo Teddy yo yo yo!

Says me to Teddy well you gotta look the part
You gotta look cool and you gotta look smart
You need the sunglasses and the shiny suit
You need the tight trousers and the cowboy boots.

I said go!
Go Teddy go go go!
Yo Teddy yo yo yo!
Go Teddy go go go!
Yo Teddy yo yo yo!

Well Teddy he's out there a struttin' his stuff
Lookin' like the Teddy the chicks love to love
But the bouncer here he looks mean and tough
Looks at Teddy full of envy, he's had about enough.

I said go!
Go Teddy go go go!
Yo Teddy yo yo yo!
Go Teddy go go go!
Yo Teddy yo yo yo!

Says bouncer to me Teddy, well ain't you the one
If you know what's good, you'll my advice son
Go back to your picnic have some teddy-bear fun
And leave these lovely ladies - now let's be movin on!

I said go!
Go Teddy go go go!
Yo Teddy yo yo yo!
Go Teddy go go go!
Yo Teddy yo yo yo!

Well Teddy wasn't one to take his advice
He didn't like the bouncer - no the bouncer wasn't nice
The next I knew was a terrible clout
One paw from Teddy and the bouncer he was out.

I said go!
Go Teddy go go go!
Yo Teddy yo yo yo!
Go Teddy go go go!
Yo Teddy yo yo yo!

So every Friday night he is King of the Club
His only bear necessity is struttin' his stuff
Forget the honey, I'm not Winnie the Pooh
No, a bear's gotta dance, that's what a bear's gotta do!

I said go!
Go Teddy go go go!
Yo Teddy yo yo yo!
Go Teddy go go go!
Yo Teddy yo yo yo!

Bimbo*

Now you can eat Bimbo
Wherever you like
You can eat it in the day
You can eat it late at night
And every time you're chewing
On this tasteless bread
The ad man's words
Go around in your head.

Bimbo, Bimbo te amor
Bimbo es mejor!

Bimbo au chocolat
Bimbo plain pan
You can't get away from this Bimbo, man!
There's Bimbo in the supermarket
Bimbo on TV
Bimbo on the billboard poster
Staring back at me.

Bimbo, Bimbo te amor
Bimbo es mejor!

Bimbo for the kids
For Pop and for Mam
It's the kind of dullest taste
That suits everyone.
No-one knows the
Secret of the Bimbo fame
Perhaps it's not the bread

It's the Bimbo name.

Bimbo, Bimbo te amor
Bimbo es mejor!

Next time I go looking for a loaf of tasty bread
I'll remember just what the ad man said.
Never choose a bread with a catchy name
Sounds like something different
But it's Bimbo all the same!

Bimbo, Bimbo te amor
Bimbo es mejor!

*Bimbo is the most famous make of sliced bread
in Spain

Boys vs. girls

Boys - If you ever think of weeing on an express train
Then take my advice and think again.
If you're a boy the story goes like this
You're aiming as normal but then you miss.
You thought it was a bulls-eye
You thought it was the middle
But the target it moved
And you're covered in piddle.
You've yellow on your shoe
A damp patch on your pants
And if the others see you
They'll know it's not by chance.
You dry to put the blower on
To dry things up a tad
But oops! You cannot keep your balance
Things are looking bad.
I'm afraid it's the end of the line for me
I'm never ever coming out
I just wish I was a girl instead
No aim to worry about.
You can sit upon your bottom
Feel the carriage sway
Concentrate upon it madly,
Let the wee go its own way.
So girls you mustn't complain
When you can't wee amongst the pines
You wouldn't want to be a boy
And pee on railway lines.

Eat up your veg

An apple a day
Keeps the doctor away
But I say
Try a sweetie
Or a biscuit
Or a lump of cake
Or a fizzy drink
Some chips
Or a chocolate milk shake.
A can of worms
A snail
A gorilla's armpit
A cup of snot
A pint of blood
Or a barrel load of sick -
But not a sprout
A carrot
Or a cauliflower cheese,
Take my advice
Eat anything
But no more veggies
Please.

The bun fight

Now listen to the story of the bun fight
It happened on one lonely winter's night
I covered up the cakes around five o'clock
By the early morning had a riot in my shop.

The trouble it started with the Eccles cake
Complained that the jam tarts kept him awake
Sticky little strawberry got in the way
Jammin' up the pastry till the break of day.

Chorus:
Now would you believe? Yeah, yeah, yeah!
Not in your wildest dreams. Yeah, yeah, yeah!
That your chocolate éclair - Yeah, yeah, yeah!
Could fall apart at the seams. Yeah, yeah, yeah!
You know that I'm not lying
And I saw it there. Yeah, yeah, yeah!

Then the carrot cake had something to say
Said it didn't like the Eccles cake acting that way
Think you're so smart with your raison d'être
But what about my toppin' full of icing sugar?

The vanilla slice heard the carrot cake
Says you're nothing yourself, you're no great
shake
No, you need puff pastry and a little cream
Add some vanilla, I'm the cakey queen!

Chorus

Now listen Puffy Pastry said ol' chocolate fudge
I'm the King of Cakies and I'll never budge
I'm brown and I'm sickly and I'm chocolate fill
Come up and see me honey for a sweety thrill.

Now come on all of you with your fancy names
How about old Sconney here, old plainy Jane
What I lack in good looks and a tarty coverin'
I make up with my volume and a jam and cream
smotherin'

Chorus

So you see there's no end to this cakey dispute
Despite the fact that every cakey looks kinda
cute
No the truth is that there's a monster lying there
If they're lookin' for a bun fight you'd better
beware.

Chorus

Snotty nosies

Why, I looked around
And just what did I see?
Thousands of those noses
A runnin' after me.
Some black, some yellow
Some deepest green
The runniest noses
You've ever seen.
I get me a hanky
I start to wipe
But the river won't dam
I'm losing the fight.
The nose it's gushing
There's snot on every face
Someone turned the tap on
It's flooding every place.
A pool upon my hand
A sheen upon his sleeve
And now he's sucking stalactites
Between his two front teeth.
I guess we're reaching crisis
Despair, distraught, dismay
At the tissues and the hankies
You have soaked along the way
And now there's nothing more
I'm reaching for the stopcock
One sharp twist to the left and right
And I've just pulled your nose off.

Tasty

Tonight we're taking Thai home
Tomorrow it's Chinese
As well as French and Indian
We like Vietnamese.
Our tastes are truly global
We've got ourselves a wok
Sharpening the kitchen knives
We're taking on the lot.
But – how do you cook an Indian?
Sari or turban dressing
And what about the Chinese
Deep fry whole, no messing.
French, well garlic through and through
No need to add the spices.
Vietnamese and Thailander
Well, try with different rices.
Italians best in pizza dough
Tex-Mex tortilla dips
Spanish dipped in tasty tapas
And Englishman – with chips.

Dream bar

This is the chocolate bar of your dreams
No money needed – yours for free.
That flavour creamy, dreamy,
The texture smoothy, softy, silkerly.
That chocolate milky, so choclate-y
Melting, grad-u-ally
'Twixt tongue and teeth – luvverly
You are a-floating – heavenly
On clouds of white – flufferly.
And you will be
Where you will be
Swimming in celestial sea
Overcoming gravity.

My sheet

My sheet, I cling to it
With its soft cotton embrace.
Covers you with kisses
From toes to face.
A safe and snug place
To hide from anger and doubt
That lies without
On the other side of my sheet
Where weary walk
The troubled feet
Of another race
Who have no sheet, no snug place.
After a warm soak
I wrap myself in sheet and cloak
And cannot describe the peace within.
Where does the sheet end and I begin?

Cowboys and cacti (a lesson for the President)

Part One
The cowboys came riding across the plains
Looking real mean, holding the reins
Of real tough horses who looked kinda mean
Like the boys on their backs they was muscle and lean.

The cowboys came riding across the plains
Heads full of whisky, guts full of beans
Dreams full of gold on the new frontier
Thousand of them acres, one thousand head of steer.

Now the cowboys came riding right into the scrub
Where even those cowboys found going was tough
The burn of the sky, the heat of the day
The dry ground that drank all the water away.

The cowboys came riding right into the desert
The bushes had gone and the grass it had dried up
But the cowboys, nope they were never afraid
Just over the desert the promised land lay.

Still the cowboys kept riding on and on
And it seemed like the battle could never be won
And the cowboys began to hallucinate
Dream of fresh water, rivers and lakes.

The cowboys stopped riding and looked all around
No sign of life, no lifely sound
"We're gonna die here," said one to the others
Nothing to eat and not one drop of water.

The horses stopped still and fell on their knees
Longed for the shade, the grass and the trees

82

They, like the cowboys, had to come to an end
Closed their dark eyes and lay back in the sand.

The cowboys and horses they heard a strange scream
From somewhere above them, like out of a dream
"We've got you surrounded, hands high in the air!
That's it fellas you stay right there."

Don't move a muscle, don't take a breath
One false move and we'll scratch you to death
Hey fellas we're cacti, we dwell in this place
Just put down you weapons and do as we say."

"You drink the juices from out of our stems
Then you and your horses slowly turn round
Then you head back to where you came from
And never set foot in the desert again."

The cowboys did just as they were told
Drank from the cacti and made their way home
Promised the cacti – oh yes indeed!
They'd never come back to the land of their dreams.

Part 2
The cowboys went riding through their home town
Looking real sorry with their heads hung down
Their horses had a story to tell each one
And they said to the townsfolk, "Put down your gun."
Don't go across the desert where the mighty cacti
dwell
That's the cacti's own home and they're doing mighty
well
Folks we don't belong there, we gotta stay right here
Stop thinking gold and greed and the wild west
frontier.

Sure we look tough and maybe we look mean
But we need something more to reach the land of
dreams
The wise cacti they told us forget your promised land
For greedy cowboys and their steeds, things don't turn
out as they planned.

Part 3

Now the desert's silent and the cacti reign supreme
They ain't been seen around these parts, no cowboys
tough and mean
The cacti they changed history, the world's a better
place
While the men who would have conquered the
American Wild West...

...are telling Mr. President that staying home is best
Sir, secret cacti told us we got a new world dream
We're not going west and we won't venture east
Cowboys, horses, cacti – we just gotta live in peace.

Sleep on a mountain side

Under a velvet soft sky
We stopped still
And stood and watched
A sinking setting sun.
Sticking like glue
We could not move.
The last curtain call
Leaves us stranded,
We fall on feather of
Delicate moss, cotton grass.
Curled in snake coils
We reach for the rhythm
Of chirping and buzzing
And wait for daybreak
For the clean cold
Crisp clear blue sheet.

The great sweetshop robbery

Ian Adams agreed with it
Sweet shop owners had more than they needed.
We should set our little plan in motion
The greatest sweety redistribution.

Monday to Friday after school
We'd meet for manoeuvres as a rule.
We'd need to get the moves just right
We'd want to win without a fight.

We needed a line or two to say
To help us robbers get our way
We practised and practised and practised our song -
If you want justice - sing along

Hold your hands up!
Get your chocolate out!
Don't want to hear anyone
Scream or shout.
Hey mister, what is this all about?
It's a genuine sweet shop robbery
Your Mars, your Twix, your Snickers
All for me, yeah, yeah, yeah, yeaah
All for me, yeah, yeah, yeah, yeaah
All for me!

The day it came and we left our den
Stood inside the shop, two grown men
Each with a moustache and a fluffy beard -
I tell you we were looking weird.

Say mister - yeah, say mister - yeah,
This is a real gun,

We want all your sweeties,
We want to have some fun.

Hold your hands up!
Get your chocolate out!
Don't want to hear anyone
Scream or shout.
Hey mister, what is this all about?
It's a genuine sweet shop robbery
Your Mars, your Twix, your Snickers
All for me, yeah, yeah, yeah, yeaah
All for me, yeah, yeah, yeah, yeaah
All for me!

But Mr. Bateson - he was nobody's fool
Says Kids your just not acting cool!
I know exactly who you are underneath that disguise
Now run home to mummy with your plastic gunny
Before I split my sides.

But before you do - sing your song.
I just love to sing along.

Hold your hands up!
Get your chocolate out!
Don't want to hear anyone
Scream or shout.
Hey mister, what is this all about?
It's a genuine sweet shop robbery
Your Mars, your Twix, your Snickers
All for me, yeah, yeah, yeah, yeaah
All for me, yeah, yeah, yeah, yeaah
All for me!

In my day

In my day we didn't have daytime television
We had to make our own amusement,
Bashing burst balls about with bits of wood
Slide tackling each other on old tarmac
Taking ourselves off to hospital
Dripping blood, bones broken, insides out.
Yes, we know to play hard in my day
Hard and fair mind, hard and fair.
We didn't sit there waving joysticks,
Playstations and computer games.
Hey and yeah we'd only just got colour TV
And only BBC and ITV
So we spent time listening to LPs
(Big circular pieces of plastic
With fabulous pop songs on it).
We wore each other's trousers
Me and my brothers
Played out till sunset
Our parents never worried.
We holidayed in England
And put up with the rain
We'd never been on aeroplanes
Or set foot on planet Spain.
We had enough but never too much money
To buy drugs and all that malarkey.
Any road we didn't need them
What with playing, running, chasing and screaming
And laughing in great gangs
Of kids aged six to sixteen.
No-one playing by themselves

Lost in front of that screen.
We were switched on, excited,
Emotional, sad and delighted.
We weren't entertained
By videos, satellite, theme parks,
Multi-screens, McDonalds,
No we had electricity, running water
And a roof over our heads
Full stomach and a pair of shoes to stand in.
In my day when kids were kids
And grown-ups were respected
And policemen frightening people.
We left our doors open and
Our keys in the lock,
We weren't scared of anything
Except the dinosaurs who roamed the earth
In my day.

The talking turkey dinosaur

Said ever so clearly to me
From his position in the middle
Of my plate -
Listen mate
Do us a favour don't eat me
I'm breadcrumb, I'm battered
I'm cheap minced turkey.
Fatty I'll fool you to taste so good
I'm chemical extra synthetic food.
What's more, I don't roar
One hundred percent turkey, no dinosaur,
Not a bit, I'm sorry mate.
I'm a low class meal
With a high class name
But they call me brontosaurus
So you'll eat me just the same.

Rosa's toad

'Twas to be a dark night for toad
For hadn't he always been told
Never ever step on the glassy black
Of the silky smooth tarmac road.
But when the evening rains came
Toad could not resist the call of the lane
A chance to cross to the other side
A new beginning, a new life
More stones for hiding
More insects for eating
The glassy black tarmac to play on
And the whole night ahead of him.
Toad's eyes bulged even bigger,
His skin more slimy at the thought
He hopped on the tarmac and back again
He wasn't the risk-taking sort.
Off and on for half an hour
Then he made a run
Back and forth and back and forth -
Taking a chance was fun!
I'll rest here a while he thought to himself
And hide from the morning sun
Which alas for toad would never come,
His young toad life just begun.
He lay on the cool of the tarmac at night
Dreamt of luxury life by the river
And so died a happy contented toad
Under the wheels of a hit and run driver.

Cure

Give me the soothing pink
The syrup of Calpol
A wondrous drink.
For fevers, aches and broken bones
Colds and flu and runny nose
TV eyes, earache, headache
Sudden death, toothache, Calpol make
Heap big better when
You're under the weather.
Colour in the cheeks, a healthy glow
When before you looked like death warmed up
With cheeks as white as snow.
Down comes the pulse
And the temperature too
Now you can do
What you really want to do.
Like play out all day
With you mates in the park
Instead of lying half-dead
In your bed in the dark.
My parents are alternative
They take herbs and smells not pills
But when it comes to curing me
Calpol cures all ills.

Why people drive cars to shops and schools

People drive short distances
To save time so that
They can spend more seconds
Watching soaps, ironing shirts
And soaking up cyberspace.
It doesn't make sense
To waste time and walk
Since then one might
Simply think in silence
And watching soaps
Ironing shirts and
Soaking up cyberspace
Might pale into
Insignificance.

Ol' Seagull

Old seagull decided he'd
Start around six
Caw-caw-caw-cawin'
Through a hole in his beak.

I lay in my bed
I could not get to sleep
Old seagull he sing to me
Cheep, cheep, cheep, cheep.

Old seagull he swims
He flies in the air
But he always returns
To his place over there.

Old, seagull, old seagull
I'm tired of thee
My ears they do clatter
Are you laughing at me?

Well I'll have the last laugh
At your open beak
Here comes a present
Try swallow this brick!

Then there was silence
Sure what have I done?
I cried for the seagull
He'd been so much fun.

Old seagull the same
Old seagull's come back
How I love seagull
Caw, caw, caw 'tis fact!

Old seagull he swims
He flies in the air
But he always returns
To his place over there.

Old seagull he swims
He flies in the air
But he always returns
To his place over there.

Happy isn't cool

Why, oh why is it cool to look sad?
What did God do that things turned out so bad?
I'm young and fit and terminally depressed
Secretly I'd like to smile but being cool is best.
I practice in the mirror looking grim and mean
And squash the ugly smiles that threaten in
between.
I concentrate on black of war of dim and death
and hate
Mix it in the mental palette, smear it 'cross my
face.
I've a grimace for the parent, for the teacher
too,
A snarl for my best mate and indifference to you
Who tries to turn and smile at me
How un-cool can someone be?

Yes being cool is where it's at
And my sad face makes sure of that.